DAILY VAGUS NERVE

Self-Help Exercises for Anxiety, Depression and Trauma

Lucas Miller

Summary:

Introduction

Post-traumatic stress disorder (PTSD) is brought on by people who have experienced a traumatic injury or languish trouble or functional disability. Manifestations incorporate sentiments of re-encountering the horrendous mishap, keeping away from tokens of the damage, uplifted tension and excitement, and negative musings or emotions. Ongoing catastrophic events, mass shootings, psychological oppressor assaults, and urban communities under attack add to the worldwide weight of PTSD which, as indicated by a recent report, influences 4–6% of the world's population, even though most of the injuries identified with mishaps and sexual or physical savagery. Shockingly, there is no known fix, and flow medicines are not convincing for all patients. A PTSD psychopharmacology committee recently gathered and distributed their accord proclamation, calling for a quick activity to address the emergency in PTSD treatment, referring to three significant concerns.

The US FDA endorses just two medications (sertraline and paroxetine) for the treatment of PTSD. These meds decrease side effects seriousness; however, it may not create a total reduction of side effects. The subsequent concern is identified with polypharmacy. PTSD patients are recommended prescriptions to address every one of their numerous extraordinary and assorted side effects, including nervousness, trouble dozing, sexual brokenness, wretchedness, and interminable torment. The high comorbidity among PTSD and fixation gives further difficulties to pharmacotherapies.

The third significant concern is the absence of headways in the treatment of PTSD; no new prescriptions have been endorsed since 2001.

Going past side effect alleviation, the 'best quality level' way to deal with treating PTSD pathology is introduction based treatment, where patients are presented to the tokens of the injury until they figure out how to connect these prompts with wellbeing. Despite the fact that there is proof for adequacy with this methodology, not all patients react entirely to the treatment. Introduction treatment relies on the way toward stifling the adapted dread memory, which is overwhelmed by another mind that creates through rehashed exposures. The patients with nervousness issues and PTSD show weaknesses in their capacity to quench adapted feelings of dread, which could add to the advancement of scatters and may meddle with the progress in treatment. Since the memory of the injury isn't lost at the same time, but rather, upgrades through treatment based on newly learned affiliations that horrible rival alliances, the parity of the two recollections can move after some time, prompting backslide. Different difficulties incorporate the trouble in perceiving and smothering apprehension of every single molded boost and a high dropout rate, which isn't astonishing given that shirking is one of the indications of PTSD.

Numerous creature investigative labs have tried endeavors to create adjunctive medications to quicken or improve the impacts of presentationbased treatments. Spearheading work done by Michael Davis demonstrated that organization of the psychological improving medication d-cycloserine before presenting rodents to unreinforced molded signals upgraded annihilation, and he and his associates, therefore, deciphered the disclosure when they found that d-cycloserine improved the impacts of presentation treatment in patients with understandable fears. In any case, aftereffects of studies evaluating the effects of psychological enhancers as subordinates to presentation treatment are blended on account of PTSD. A conceivable clarification is that medications given before introduction treatment sessions risk fortifying negative affiliations if presentation produces nervousness. Anxiolytic drugs have been attempted in light of proof that these medications ought to improve decency and decrease the tension reaction during the introduction. Nonetheless, results show that anxiolytic medications don't improve the impacts of presentation treatment. One clarification is that the uneasiness reaction is required for accomplishment in introduction treatment since patients must learn not to fear their own dread reaction. Similarly, just as stress can improve the capacity of horrendous mishaps, the tension reaction may upgrade the combination of the termination memory.

Predictable with this, anxiolytic medications will, in general, hinder memory combination. A perfect deal would take advantage of the systems that improve the union of horrendous recollections so as to advance elimination recollections that are similarly as solid, at the same time bypassing or maintaining a strategic distance from the aversive pressure reaction.

Developing proof proposes that vagus nerve incitement (VNS) might be a gainful extra to introduction based treatments through its blending of definite improvement of memory combination and neural versatility. Enthusiasm for the vagus nerve (the tenth cranial nerve) as a neuromodulator originates from a long strand of research demonstrating that the vagus nerve fills in as an extension between the fringe autonomic sensory system and the cerebrum. It flags the mind during times of elevated thoughtful movement, advancing quick stockpiling of recollections that are significant for endurance. As a vital aspect of the parasympathetic sensory system, initiation of the vagus nerve neutralizes the thoughtful pressure reaction.

VNS upgrades memory in rodents and people, proposing that blending VNS with an unreinforced introduction to adapted signals may improve the union of the elimination memory. Predictable with this theory, we found that VNS upgraded the elimination of molded dread in rodents. Ample proof shows that VNS advances neural versatility, particularly when it is combined with preparing, and this impact includes VNS regulation of the locus coeruleus noradrenergic framework. We have watched pliancy impacts in the termination related infralimbic prefrontal cortex – basolateral amygdala pathway in the wake of blending VNS with a presentation to unreinforced molded prompts, proposing that VNS-improved elimination might be hearty, enduring, and less vulnerable to backslide. In an ongoing report, we found that VNS improved termination of molded dread in a rodent model of PTSD. These rodents express a considerable lot of the biomarkers and conduct phenotypes that are related to PTSD and, significantly, they are impervious to the elimination of molded dread. We found that the VNS organization during elimination sessions switched this termination disability and counteracted the arrival of fear. VNS-treated rodents likewise performed better on the trial of tension, excitement, evasion, and social association's weeks later, demonstrating that inversion of the elimination hindrance meant enhancements in other PTSD indications.

Moreover, interminable, unpaired VNS, as is utilized in the treatment of epilepsy and despondency, improved execution on the Hamilton Anxiety Scale in individual patients with tension issues, and diminished uneasinesslike conduct in rodents. The impacts of VNS on termination in our examinations are not seen when the VNS is managed 30 min to 1 h in the wake of preparing. In this way, VNS alone isn't adequate to decrease the dread reaction. These discoveries recommend that VNS may diminish nervousness, however, matching explicit pliancy and memory tweak is vital for elimination upgrade. Our ongoing, unpublished findings show that rodents are bound to investigate the open arms of a rodent raised in addition to labyrinth following getting VNS, proposing that VNS produces a powerful anxiolytic impact. Moreover, corticosterone levels expanded radically in trick treated rodents following testing on the raised in addition to the labyrinth, however, such an expansion was not seen in VNS-treated rodents. This work ought to be imitated in different settings, yet it is an empowering initial move toward distinguishing an assistant treatment that may improve decency and adequacy in presentation based treatments.

What is Vagus Nerve

It is a parcel of sensory and motor fibers. It begins in the brain stem and interacts with the heart, lungs, and gut. It continues to spread out and interact with other major organs such as the liver, gallbladder, spleen, and more.

Our involuntary nerve center is boosted and regulates insensate body operations. It monitors your heart rate, breathing, food digestion, and sweating. Our blood pressure and blood glucose are balanced. It helps the function of the kidney, the discharge of testosterone and bile, the release of saliva is stimulated, controls taste releases tears, and is a major key in orgasms in women and fertility issues (Ropp, 2017).

Approximately 80 percent of the nerve fibers transmit information by way of

four "lanes" of the nerve. In the opposite direction, the fifth lane is simultaneously bringing signs from the brain through the body.

The nerve begins in the brain stem, extends down the neck and into the chest where it splits into left and right Vagus. Tens of thousands of nerve fibers that each "road" is composed of branches out into all the major organs in the body.

To say that the Vagus nerve has a lot to do with how our involuntary nerve center is powered is an understatement. It has been noted that "if we were without the Vagus nerve, many major functions of the body that keep us alive would not be maintained." In order to have your Vagus functioning at optimum levels, it needs to be activated.

Acetylcholine, the neurotransmitter stimulates muscle contractions and is used by the Vagus nerve. This allows signals to be moved from one place to another and stimulates various organs. Acetylcholine production can be interfered with by substances such as Botox and the heavy metal mercury. Botox is a substance that can interfere with the Vagus nerve. Another problem is mercury - it blocks acetylcholine.

What happens if your Vagus nerve is not functioning properly? For some of us, the solution may be to have it electronically stimulated.

The FDA has approved the use of vagus nerve stimulation in treating two different chronic conditions. People who have epilepsy or have an autistic child may find that this route is the most beneficial way to stimulate the Vagus nerve to treat and improve these illnesses. Scientists have recognized the possibility of stimulating the Vagus nerve with an electronic implant that is activated with a magnetic strip. Chronic conditions such as epilepsy and autism have had FDA approval to implant this device for treatment. Those with chronic conditions report great results having their Vagus nerve stimulated many times each day.

People with chronic pain and stiffness and who could barely get out of bed are seeing amazing results. They're able to go on long walks, swim, and even dance again. The stimulation of the Vagus nerve is aiding the body in doing what it's supposed to do – heal itself.

When our nervous system functions at optimum levels, we feel great. However, Vagus nerve damage or low vagal tone is more the norm. Even small changes to the Vagus nerve can exhibit results that are impressive. There are several studies being conducted to prove the stimulation of the nerve is a useful way to treat more chronic diseases. Whether the treatment is electronic or non-invasive, stimulations proving to be a non-medicinal way to have diseases show improvement. However, what about stimulating the Vagus nerve ourselves? What can we do to activate it? But before we get into how to activate it, a look at what causes the nerve to become damaged is called. Fixing what's broken doesn't work if you don't address and fix what caused it to be broken in the first place.

Vagal Dysfunction

Vagal dysfunction can bring a myriad of problems that can disrupt the normal flow of the body and introduce chronic disease and illness.

The Vagus nerve has quite a few conditions that have been linked or are being researched at this time for a link to this nerve. These issues can range from minor conditions to serious, more significant issues.

Quite a few people will have a vasovagal reaction eventually because of the overstimulation or stress of the Vagus nerve. Some reasons and results linked to the Vagus nerve being irritated or damaged include:

- Obesity
- Hormonal imbalance
- Constant stress and anxiety
- Alcohol addiction
- Diabetes
- Cancer
- Spicy foods
- IBS (Irritable Bowel Syndrome)
- Insomnia
- Chronic Fatigue
- Chronic inflammation
- Migraine headaches
- Alzheimer's disease
- Poor blood circulation
- Leaky gut
- Mood disorders

- Vitamin deficiency
- Depression Tinnitus

So, if you're overweight, are stressed and anxious on a consistent basis, overdo it with alcohol, have developed diabetes, eat spicy foods, are constantly fatigued, and can identify with many of the other causes or reactions you may be having, your Vagus nerve is probably irritated. These conditions are due to the inability to switch from the sympathetic responses and reestablish balance and calmness in your body.

Damage of the Vagus Nerve
A range of symptoms can manifest due to damage to the Vagus nerve. The main reason for this is because the nerve is so long and affects many organs of the body. (Seladi-Schulman, 2018)

- A hoarse voice or wheezy

- Loss of gag reflex

- Trouble drinking liquids

- Difficulty speaking

- Decreased production of stomach acid

- Vomiting or nausea

- Pain or abdominal bloating

- Testing the Vagus Nerve

A doctor may check the gag reflex to test the Vagus nerve. The doctor may use a cotton swab to tickle both sides of the back of the throat. Normally, this should cause a person to gag. If they don't, this may indicate a problem with the Vagus nerve. There are ways that can help to revitalize the Vagus nerve. Stimulation of the nerve can be a help for your body. Studies have been done to exhibit how important the Vagus nerve is and how it interfaces with so many of the body's organs.

The Vagus nerve furnishes us to react to psychological, physical, and emotional symptoms that come from a lack of balance in the body and might be the key to improving your health.

When you perform vagal nerve stimulation, there are major improvements health-wise, including the relief of many autoimmune illnesses and an overall feel-better effect.

The Vagus nerve works well when it is strong and has a high vagal tone. If you are dealing with many of the named irritants and results linked to the vagal nerve, the vagal tone is low. Vagal tone is an indication of the condition you are in. For example, people who exercise on a regular basis, athletes, and those who practice yoga or other types of physical activity will exhibit a higher vagal tone.

Adversely, people who are alcoholics or drink far beyond legal limits, along with people who are bedridden or don't exercise regularly, have lower vagal tone. You may have a low vagal tone if your mother also had a low vagal tone during her pregnancy with you. She may have been stressed, anxious, or angry during the pregnancy. It's possible the low vagal tone was passed down to you.

In order to increase your vagal tone, you need to work it out, just like exercising the body and continue to activate it. You don't need to do an elaborately long workout – 15 to 20 minutes each day would be good. The more you do, it would be better, but if you're doing daily stimulations of the Vagus nerve, you're doing okay.

Activating the Vagus Nerve

Most people envision the Vagus nerve to be one thin cord reaching from the brain stem to the gut. Actually, it is a nerve that extends down both sides of the body and is a branch of the shaggy, meandering nerve that connects to most of the major organs like a system of cables or roots. (Zimmerman, 2019)

The Vagus nerve is responsible for the mind-body connection, its role as a go-between between thinking and feeling.

Stimulating the Vagus nerve has an impactful effect on lowering the heart rate. This is what relaxes us. Our Vagus nerve is receiving information from the way we breathe and sends it to the brain and the heart the message our breathing signifies.

The more we activate it with deep breathing, the more we negate the effects of the sympathetic nervous system. Instead of feeling stressed and anxious, we feel calm and relaxed.

The heart slows, and we relax when we breathe slowly, but when we breathe quickly, our heart rate increases, and we feel anxious or amped. Vagal activity is at its highest, and the heart rate is at its lowest when you exhale.

Researchers found that the most calming way to breathe is six times a minute.

Five seconds inhale, five seconds exhale.

This style of slow breathing is also what practitioners of meditation naturally drift into with mantras they recite slowly. Each time you repeat a meditation mantra, your breathing naturally coordinates your breathing at six times a minute. (Zimmerman, 2019)

There are ways to measure the vagal tone – finding out how strong, healthy, and functioning the nerve is. Measuring the heart rate variability (HRV) is a substitute way to measure vagal tone (the other way would be open chest surgery).

The amount that the heart rate fluctuates between breaths in when it speeds up naturally and breathe out when it slows down is heart rate variability. Thus the heart rate increases when we inhale and decreases when we exhale, and the difference between the two rates measure vagal tone.

People who are physically active such as athletes, usually have a higher vagal tone, and those who have a sedentary lifestyle with little to no exercise and, surprisingly, astronauts who spend time in no-gravity situations are known to have low vagal tone. There are many ways to stimulate the Vagus nerve. You can laugh, sing, chant, hum, gargle, meditate, do full-body exercising, breathing exercises, or engage in sound-related activities such as listening to music or white noise.

These are just a few activities recommended for stimulation. Splashing cold water on your face or taking a full-body rinse with cold water after a shower is another way of stimulating the Vagus nerve.

Mild exercise and general full-body exercise will increase fluids in the gut, which will stimulate the Vagus nerve. The muscles at the back of the throat will be worked by laughing and singing, also activating the nerve and sounding OM while practicing meditation.

Activating the Vagus nerve encompasses sound. Sound is a major alternative in healing, as well as music. They are a great way to stimulate the Vagus nerve in a non-invasive, natural manner.

Dancing is another physical activity that releases endorphins, reduces stress, and causes our body to have a feeling of optimism, happiness, and calm. It also incorporates two key elements – sound and movement, which are good for Vagus stimulation.

Dance, as movement therapy, reduces anxiety, helps people suffering from depression, and those who have anxiety in social settings. It increases strength in muscles and improves flexibility offering a better range of motion.

It also increases core strength, thus improving coordination, balance, and posture.

Aside from being a good overall exercise, it stimulates the brain helping to reduce feelings of loneliness, memory (remembering dance steps) recognizing beat, synchronizing music with movement, and feeling the rhythm of the music.

How the Vagus Nerve Affects Anxiety

Anxiety is something that every person will experience in life, and it is entirely reasonable. We feel anxiety when we go to a job interview or on our first date. However, when you suffer from an anxiety disorder, things can be very different.

It might start with a sense of dread, and you may begin to feel fearful or irritable, you can't make it go away no matter what you do. An anxiety disorder is different from merely feeling anxious every now and then. Those that suffer from an anxiety disorder struggle with day to day tasks such as going to work or checking out at the grocery store. They may not be able to socialize or be part of a relationship.

Types of Anxiety

As stated, there are many different types of anxiety; however, there are only six major types of anxiety disorder. They are PTSD or post-traumatic stress disorder, generalized anxiety disorder, social anxiety disorder, OCD or obsessive-compulsive disorder, panic disorder, and finally, phobia.

PTSD, as most people know post-traumatic stress disorder, occurs as a result of someone having a life-threatening or traumatizing event take place in their life. The person could experience agitation, nightmares, random flashbacks or recollections, paranoia, and evasion of any circumstance that would remind them of the event.

OCD or obsessive-compulsive disorder is something that we hear thrown around a lot, but many people really do not understand. OCD is much more than just wanting to clean your house every day or make sure that the pictures are straight. It is compulsions that the patient has no control over, such as turning the light on and off 36 times before they are physically able to leave the room, and if the light is turned off 35 times, they have to start over.

Generalized anxiety disorder is also known as GAD, happens when a patient worries so much or has so many fears that they are unable to accomplish tasks for the day to day life. They may also feel that something terrible is always going to happen no matter what. When someone is a worrywart, they are demonstrating symptoms of GAD. They have no reason to feel anxious, they have no history of bad things happening to them, but the fear is so intense that they are not able to focus on anything else.

Social anxiety disorder is when a person has an extreme fear of negativity when they are in public or a fear of being humiliated in public. Someone who is excessively bashful may be suffering from a social anxiety disorder; however, it may become even more extreme than that. Sometimes the person will also withdraw from their families. They are so afraid that they do not want to interact with people at all. Those who have stage fright are often used as an example of what social anxiety looks like.

We have all heard of phobias, a fear that is exaggerated concerning something that would or could not pose any type of danger or threat to the person. A hatred is very intense, and people will go to extremes to ensure that they avoid the thing that they are afraid of. In reality, this is only reinforcing the fear; however, many people have phobias of heights, specific animals, flying, or of the dark.

All of the different types of anxiety disorders can be placed in one of these major types. While they are all anxiety disorders, it is crucial to know the difference because they all affect the person differently and can affect different areas of their lives.

Symptoms of Anxiety

Anxiety not only affects a person's mental health, but it can impact them physically as well. While we know that there are short term effects of anxiety, what many people do not know is that there are short term effects as well.

Symptoms of anxiety can include:

- Feeling fearful, nervous, or even tense
- Feeling restless
- Suffering from panic attacks
- Increased heart rate
- Increased breathing rate
- Shaking
- Sweating
- Weakness or fatigue
- Dizziness
- Trouble concentrating
- Insomnia
- Digestive issues and nausea

- Problems with body temperature (such as feeling far colder or hotter than is usual)
- Pains in the chest
- Feeling the need to display certain behaviors in order to reduce the anxiety that is felt

Moreover, anxiety affects the body in many other ways, which can actually lead to chronic illnesses.

When our bodies feel stress, they respond by telling our bodies that we are going to have to flee or fight. This is known as the fight or flight response. At this point, our bodies also release both adrenalin and cortisol, which many people know as the stress hormones.

While the fight or flight response is constructive if you are hiking through the woods and come upon a bear, it is not that useful when it happens during a job interview or on a date. It is also unhealthy for us to remain in this state for an extended period of time. When we are exposed to cortisol and adrenaline for too long, they can actually cause damage to our bodies.

When we are faced with anxiety in a stressful situation, it is normal for our breathing to become faster and shallow. It allows our body to take in more oxygen so that it is prepared if we have to fight or run. If this happens all of the time, as it does when a person is suffering from an anxiety disorder, they may continuously feel lightheaded, weak, faint, or dizzy.

Anxiety can also cause our heart rates to increase as well as increase the amount of blood that is pumped through our bodies. This happens as our body is preparing to fight or run because the extra blood is going to provide our muscles with extra nutrients and oxygen. At this point, our blood vessels will also narrow, which causes hot flashes.

Our bodies begin to sweat in order to cool down, and if a person is suffering from anxiety, they may feel freezing all of the time.

After looking at what anxiety does to the cardiovascular system, it is easy to understand how an anxiety disorder could cause heart problems. Studies have actually shown that those who suffer from anxiety disorders are actually at a higher risk of developing heart disease in life.

Anxiety will boost your immune system in the short term; however, it is possible for it to have the opposite effect on the body when exposure is prolonged.

Cortisol will stop the body from releasing histamine into the body when it goes into the fight or flight reaction, and this impairs the body's immune system responses. However, it has been found that people who suffer from chronic anxiety disorders are more likely to catch the flu, a cold, or other viruses. Therefore, it is imperative that if you are suffering from any type of chronic anxiety disorder, you focus on boosting your immune system as much as possible.

When our bodies go into the fight or flight response, processes that are nonessential for survival stop, this means that digestion stops. On top of that, because adrenaline reduces blood flow to the stomach and causes it to relax, digestion is affected. Because of this, people who suffer from chronic anxiety disorders may suffer from the feeling of a churning stomach, nausea, diarrhea, or they may simply lose their appetite.

Some studies have linked anxiety, depression, and stress to IBS (irritable bowel syndrome).

Anxiety can also cause a person to feel as if they need to urinate more often. This is very common when a person has a phobia. It is believed that the body loses control of the bladder functions when the person suffers from anxiety because it is easier for the body to run from the threat if the bladder is empty. However, many scientists are still unsure why the urge to urinate happens; yet, they have many different theories.

Suffering from anxiety can have many adverse short-term effects, but it can also have long-term effects as well. Those that suffer from chronic anxiety may also have insomnia, digestive issues, depression, and difficulty in socializing, at work, or at school, substance abuse, thoughts of suicide, and a loss of interest in sex or other things that they once enjoyed. These long-term effects can be life-altering and very difficult for a person do deal with. Being a female. It is more likely for a female to suffer from anxiety than a male.

- A history of substance abuse.
- Having to deal with a lot of stress for an extended period of time, from home, finance, and/or work
- Having a parent that suffers from anxiety.
- Suffering a traumatic experience in your life.
- Having a chronic medical condition such as cardiovascular disease.
- Use of certain medications.

- Having one or more other mental health disorders.

In order to be diagnosed with an anxiety disorder, you have to see a doctor. They are the only ones that can tell you what is really going on. They will be able to provide you with the medication, support, and information about lifestyle changes you can make to feel better.

You can then focus on stimulating the vagus nerve to improve even more.

Anxiety and the Vagus Nerve

When the vagus nerve is stimulated, it causes a response, which reduces stress. Vagus nerve stimulation helps to reduce the heart rate as well as blood pressure. It also stimulates functioning in different parts of the brain as well as digestion, which allows us to feel more relaxed. This is all known as the vagal response.

Simply put, the vagal response is what happens when the vagus nerve is stimulated. When the nerve is stimulated, it helps to reduce anxiety. Amazingly yoga masters were using these techniques long before scientists even knew about the vagal response.

Researchers have found that by stimulating the vagus nerve regularly anxiety, as well as stress, can be reduced. On top of this, it can also help reduce the symptoms or even neutralize COPD, asthma, and heart disease.

This should provide us with some comfort, at least. These researchers are quickly learning that not only is our physical health entirely in our control, but our mental health is as well. Studies have shown that people who suffer from mental disorders, as well as chronic illnesses such as COPD, actually benefit from vagus nerve stimulation.

There is actual science to back up the vagal response. We talked just about the fight or flight response and how it can put a person on edge. This is the same response that you feel when a person cuts you off while you are driving or when the cashier can't seem to ring up your order right no matter how many times she tries.

This response has helped to keep the human race alive over the years, but as we learned, it can also cause a lot of damage when it is experienced too often. It is then when we do not feel that we are ever really able to relax that we need to start stimulating the vagus nerve.

While stimulating the vagus nerve may sound like it is going to be very complicated, the truth is that it really is not that hard. The good news is that it also gets easier the more that you do it. We are going to talk about how you can stimulate your vagus nerve, but let me give you a little bit of a heads up.

If you can breathe, you can.

Body Stress and Vagus Nerve

Stress is a natural way of reaction to change that the body has to go through. A person is stressed when they face conflicting thoughts or when they feel threatened. If you are in a situation where you think that your life is in danger, you are likely to experience stress. Stress is accompanied by varied physical, emotional, and mental responses. When you are afraid of something or worried about something, the body will prompt specific actions to take place naturally.

Although stress is a normal part of life, it brings varied ups and downs. It is not possible to take care of your nerves if you are always afraid. As a matter of fact, any time stress kicks in, and you should let the nervous system take full control. You may experience pressure from your thoughts, your body, or the environment. In either case, the vagus nerve will directly be affected.

As we have already mentioned above, any activity that leads to either direct or indirect stimulation of the vagus nerve may affect its health. If you are always stressed, the chances are that you may continuously keep on hurting your vagus nerve. We have seen that chronic inflammation only occurs after a long time of natural rehabilitation. If the body keeps on trying to rehabilitate worn-out tissues due to injuries, it will eventually lead to inflammation. The same case applies to stress. If you continuously experience stress, you are likely to stimulate the vagus nerve to such an extent that it is impossible to recover. But how exactly does body stress relate to the vagus nerve?

Any time you are under stress, you suffer from anxiety or panic attacks. Although the symptoms of either anxiety or panic attacks are not visible, it is clear that people who suffer stress may experience some form of anxiety. The brain is programmed to respond to such stressful situations by producing CRF hormones. Although the brain naturally produces such hormones, stressful situations lead to increased production of the hormones. The CRFs travel through the hypothalamus to the pituitary glands, where they cause the release of another hormone, known as ACTH. This hormone consequently travels through the bloodstream to the adrenal glands. This leads to the stimulation of cortisol and adrenal reaction, which helps protect the boy from stress. As you can see, this process of stress protection is long and directly affects your vagus nerve. When we are suffering from stress, we are likely to get deep into a state of depression if the vagus nerve and the brain get overwhelmed.

Stress and depression have all been linked with inflammatory brain response. In other words, the process of responding to stress puts the brain under extreme pressure, leading to injuries and inflammation. In other cases, the same applies to the vagus nerve. As the nerve is exposed to the stress of trying to deal with the anxious situation, it is common for the nerve to experience injuries.

Such injuries attract the natural healing process of the body, which eventually results in inflammation. Even though the body naturally fights injuries, continued stress can lead to the constant production of hormones, which ultimately leads to actions that may cause stress to the vagus nerve.

Chronic stress can also lead to an increase in the production of glutamate in the brain. The output of glutamate may directly affect the brain and, as a result, affect the vagus nerve. For instance, glutamate is a neurotransmitter that causes migraines and depression when produced in excess. When you are under stress, it is common for the brain to initiate the production of this neurotransmitter. To protect yourself from such conditions and to ensure that you preserve your vagus nerve from any damage, ensure that you reduce stressful moments in your life. There are many ways of dealing with stress, including meditation, singing, dancing, among others. Such options will help you deal with stress and reduce the pressure on your brain. By acting to reduce pressure on your head, you respond to protect the brain and the vagus nerve as a whole.

In one research conducted by medical students from Ohio State University, it was revealed that when individual animals are put under excess pressure, they react by producing high levels of cortisol. The high degree of cortisol provided tries to reduce the volume of the hippocampus. The fact that a person is under pressure only means that they reduce their chances of having a sober brain. If you are struggling with stress, the chances are that you may not be able to concentrate or keep memories. It is essential to ensure that you reduce your levels of stress so that you focus on other aspects of life. If you do not pay much attention to your health and try to minimize the stress associated with your life situations, the chances are that you may end up living a life that painful.

All the factors that affect your brain are also impactful to your vagus nerve. Stress does not only change your mind, but it also affects your nervous system. The vagus nerve may completely fail if you keep on undergoing episodes of stress on a daily basis. The inflammation of the vagus nerve may further lead to other health complications. Swelling means that the nerve is not functioning to the maximum. A simple problem, such as inflammation, may lead to digestive and hearing problems. If the case advances, the entire vagus nerve may be affected and hence affect the autonomic nervous system.

Blood Pressure and Heart Rate

Another factor that may lead to the inflammation of the vagus nerve is blood pressure. The human body is designed to maintain a certain level of blood flow. This means that there must be signal transmission from the heart to the brain that coordinates the blood flow. The flow of the blood depends on the heart rate and the constriction of blood vessels. If blood vessels are constricted, the heart will be forced to pump the blood a lot faster so as to achieve equal distribution of blood to all body parts. In the same way, if the blood vessels are lost, the heart rate has to reduce to some extent. The vagus nerve is at the center of all the operations that affect the functioning of the heart.

Vagus nerve stimulation devices have been used for various medical purposes for more than 30 years. These devices are either implanted or used externally. Some of the joint implants are devices that range in 1 to 3.5 mA. These devices are mainly designed to influence heart rate and blood pressure. Some of the diseases that these devices aim to control include epilepsy and heart diseases. With that said, it is evident that stimulation of the vagus nerve has a significant effect on the blood pressure and heart rate.

Research shows that most of the devices used in vagus nerve stimulation, either use mechanical pressure application or automated electromagnetic waves. In the early 1800s, the data collected from such devices was vital in evaluating the overall health of the vagus nerve. Data such as the

Electrocardiogram (ECG), heart rate (HR), and blood pressure (BP) were all evaluated. However, modern-day medical applications focus tends to be on the performance of the device rather than the wellbeing of the nerve. Over the years, most device manufacturers have opted to design invasive devices that do not give out data as it was initially. This does not mean that the devices used for vagus nerve stimulation are defective in any way. The main concern would be a case where the device was causing overstimulation, resulting in fatigue and injuries to the nerve.

It is recommended to use the non-invasive vagus nerve gadgets. Wearable such as the hand and thump pressure tools are much safer. Today, some manufacturers are reverting to the traditional options of belt and hand pressure. In either case, you must ensure that the gadget you chose to use has been approved and received a clean bill of health. Understanding that any stimulating device is only supposed to help you enhance activities that are already taking place will also help you understand that overstimulation may mess up with the natural processes. The human body is made to run naturally and provide internal solutions to internal problems. This explains why the vagus nerve has to defend itself from injuries. In the case of an injury, the nerve must initiate a process of self-recovery. In this process of recovery, the damages caused to the body or to the nerves must be resolved.

If you choose to use a device that regulates your blood pressure, you must ensure that it does not go beyond the required. Overstimulation of the vagus nerve will obviously lead to excessive production of some enzymes. The parasympathetic activities of the nerve are awakened during a moment when the body should be acting in the opposite direction. Although the ultimate result of reducing heart rate may be achieved, it is still expensive and painful to experience some complications associated with the stimulation. If you want to stimulate your vagus nerve for the sake of reducing blood pressure and heart rate, only do it selectively. It should not be something you do daily.

Vagus Nerve and Depression

When people think of mental health issues, the two that come to mind are typically anxiety and depression. Depression is the other most common mental health issue around the world, and many people suffer from it. It is estimated that somewhere around 15% of people will experience depression, either acute or chronic, at some point in their lives.

This disorder can be debilitating. It can be exhausting. It can be draining, and it can be destructive. It can lead to so many different problems, and that can be a primary reason you would benefit from trying to solve the problem altogether. Instead of continuing to stress about the issue, you can defeat the problem.

Defining Depression

Depression itself is the feeling of negativity and hopelessness that people sometimes feel. It is a period in which there is a lack of interest in the world around you. You can feel like you do not want to engage with other people. You find that anything you used to be interested in is no longer compelling. You do not want to do anything at all oftentimes, and that can sometimes really just make the problem worse.

Depression can be debilitating for these people. Especially when severe, people who suffer from depression can find they do not have the energy for anything at all. They feel slow, sleepy, even if they cannot sleep. They feel stuck and unhappy. Even the activities that once brought them joy in life are no longer enjoyable, and they find that they cannot do anything about it. This is a significant problem for people; it can really hold them back. Depression is most often characterized by the following symptoms:

- You cannot regulate your mood up and regularly. Your attitude is frequently or always down, and you cannot figure out how to bring it back up, no matter how hard you may try.

- Your appetite has fluctuated dramatically, and you either eat more often now, or you do not want to eat at all.

- You struggle to sleep, or you sleep regularly. Either way, you always feel exhausted.

- Your mood is usually low, and you can find that you become very irritable sometimes.

- You are permanently fatigued; you cannot get yourself to move around because your body is just that exhausted that frequently. • You struggle to really focus on what matters to you. You cannot concentrate on the most critical aspects of your life, and you feel like your mood is endlessly dull and foggy.

- You do not have an interest in anything at all, even when they used to bring you joy.

- You feel worthless, or like you do nothing but bring the world down.

- You may fixate on the idea of death or suicide.

Depression and the Vagus Nerve

Remember, when the body feels that something is entirely futile, it shuts itself off; it stops trying to continue moving forward. It finds there is no reason to stay, so it begins to shut down and slow down. When you go into a frozen state, this is what happens. Your body dulls your mind, and your concentration struggles. You lose interest and responsiveness. You feel like you cannot move at all, or like moving or doing anything at all would take far too much effort out of your life.

The vagus nerve, when it is overactive, can trigger what is known as a parasympathetic shutdown. This is the freeze response. It is a primitive response to fear, developed long before mammals developed their more modern, nuanced fight or flight system. It is believed that depression, at or at least, certain kinds of depression, may be linked to this.

There are many types of depression that can be found to be resistant to just about all treatment options—these people are known to have treatmentresistant depression, and yet, stimulating the vagus nerve has been shown to help these people begin to get back to their old routine.

It may also be the case that depression is related to inflammation, especially if swelling is treated when you stimulate the vagus nerve. Nevertheless, regardless of whether depression caused by the vagus nerve in the same way that anxiety was, one thing is known for sure—depression can be managed with the stimulation of the vagus nerve.

We are going to consider three methods that you can use to begin fighting off depression. We are going to look at probiotics—these are relevant to the vagus nerve thanks to the prominent role that the vagus nerve plays in the digestive system and the digestive system's leading role in the production of serotonin—which happens to be one of the ways that we can treat depression. We will take a look at socialization to help bring the vagus nerve back to a sense of normalcy, and finally, we will take a look at meditation.

Probiotics to Stimulate the Vagus Nerve

Every digestive system is jam-packed with bacteria. It lines most of your digestive tract, allowing your body to mainly digesting the food within your guts. The good bacteria you want to have in your intestines are known as probiotics. These are found already in many naturally fermented foods or other foods that are cultured. Take a look at the yogurt label by the time you are at the store—you may see that it is labeled as having live culture. That live culture is all of the bacteria that you can eat and then seed into your digestive system.

When you do this, you can permanently boost the power of your digestive system. Even better, however, is the fact the digestive system can realty influence your mind. Having the right gut biome is absolutely essential when it comes to being able to function accordingly. If you want to be able to perform, you must have the right kinds of bacteria to create the right types of hormones your body will need.

In particular, Lactobacillus Rhamnosus and Bifidobacterium Longum are both associated with being able to help with stress hormones. They aid in the uptake of serotonin, and they also create positive changes to the GABA, a vital neurotransmitter for general regulation. When you do not have enough GABA in your body, it may impact your mood.

While science is still attempting to determine the exact details, it is believed when you do not have enough GABA, and you could end up suffering from anxiety, mood disorders (including depression), epilepsy, and chronic pain. For this reason, it is incredibly essential for you to recognize that the gut bacteria absolutely do impact the mind, and you need to ensure you honor that.

By taking probiotics with both Lactobacillus Rhamnosus and Bifidobacterium Longum, you can ensure that your body is going to have more of those proper bacteria that it will need to not only regulate the mood but also help with the vagus nerve as well. There have been studies done that have shown that mice actually tend to show fewer symptoms of anxiety and depression when they are given these necessary probiotics, and it is believed this is due to the vagus nerve.

Socialization to Stimulate the Vagus Nerve

Once again, we come right back to the social nervous system, the proposed method through which the vagus nerve regulates the way in which we socialize. It has been found that socialization is one of the most significant ways to reduce stress, and this makes sense. Think about it—we are social creatures. If you want to alleviate stress, you need to be around people you love and care about. This socialization can leave you feeling fulfilled and better than ever.

In particular, many therapies also entertain the idea that to treat depression, you must be willing to go out on a limb and force the point. Many of them say the only way to get moving again with your own anxiety or depression is to make sure you go out. You have to sort of reboot the mind into seeing it as enjoyable and beneficial—sound familiar?

When you suffer from depression, you oftentimes do not want to do anything at all, and yet, going out there and actively beginning to stimulate your vagus nerve through being out and exposed to other people is one of the most effective manners that you can use. You need to be able to recognize the ways you can spend that time with people and how getting out there can slowly but surely begin to engage your vagus nerve.

This does not mean you have to go out to a party tonight; instead, take it slowly. Allow yourself, too, little by little, is to better cope with the way that you are behaving. Over time, you will find you are better able to focus. Over time, you will find that this time you spend out and about is worth it. You will feel like, at the end of the day, you can, and you will be able to do everything you need to do.

Get up and get out, get moving, and be social. Even if you just spend a few minutes with someone every day, having a conversation with them at the coffee shop as you wait for your order, you are still engaging with other people, and as they join with you, you will find that, little by little, you will be able to get back to functioning. You will be able to get back to feeling whole within your own body again.

Meditation to Stimulate the Vagus Nerve

Finally, the last method we are going to consider in terms of what you can do with yourself to stimulate the vagus nerve for depression is to take a look at the ways in which you can meditate. Meditation is an incredibly powerful state of mind, and it has been found to activate those same areas within the brain that are triggered by the vagus nerve as well, implying that the two are related.

When you meditate, you are entering a quiet, stable state in which you are able to relax and focus on the way in which you are feeling. You focus on the clarity and the peace within yourself, and in doing so, you are able to slowly but surely seek solace within yourself.

Meditation is something people sometimes resist, but the truth of the matter is it is actually surprisingly robust. You do not have to go out and suddenly let go of anything you enjoy to get out there and meditate. On the contrary, you can usually do it anywhere for any amount of time, with very little commitment required. All you will need is yourself and a quiet place to rest, uninterrupted, and left alone to enjoy the peace and quiet within yourself.

- Begin by finding a beautiful, quiet place for yourself where you can relax without intervention. Make sure that it is somewhere you will be able to better focus without any distractions.

- Take a deep breath in and hold it. Then, breathe out. Repeat this process, getting used to the way your breath feels.

- Find a position that you are comfortable sitting within. It could be any position at all; it does not have to be any particular one. All that matters is you are comfortable in it.

- Slowly shift your focus to your breathing. Let yourself continue to focus on just your breath at this point, paying attention to the air coming in and out of your lungs.

- Any time that you feel your attention leave your breathing, you must quietly and gently shift it back, free from any judgment and free from any concern.

- Remain in this state for as long as you feel comfortable, preferably at least five minutes.

Activating the Vagus Nerve and Exercises

The methods presented in this topic have been practiced since ancient times. However, given that they have zero side effects and bring about an improvement in the quality of your life, you have nothing to lose when it comes to following them.

Furthermore, it would be remiss of me not to present these exercises since all of them are talked about quite a lot. So in the interest of giving you a wellrounded look at how you can stimulate the vagus nerve, let's dive into these ancient practices.

Breathing Techniques

Humming

A dull hum can get your vagus nerve up and running. The trick is to go all out with your hum and to let your inhibitions go. It isn't so much the depth of your hum or the pitch but the degree with which you can let go. Make it as deep or as shallow as you want. The theory behind this is that the vibrations in your throat and chest will stimulate the vagus nerve since it passes through these areas of your body.

So why should you let go entirely and hum? Well, this is just to get you to give it everything you've got. Besides, everyone is different, and your vagus nerve's tuning will be different from that of others. This is why there is no standard or scale in terms of the vibrational frequency you need to hit in order to stimulate the central system.

Conscious Breathing

In the depths of my depression, if someone asked me to observe my breath, I would have thrown something at them. However, the simple act of keeping your breath has the effect of slowing it down. There are some claims that the vagus nerve is activated when your breathing slows down to seven breaths per minute.

There's no doubt that simple observation can help calm you down and will help you become more grounded in the present. There are considerable benefits to this.

Valsalva Technique

This technique is carried out by pushing your breath against a closed airway. Inhale once profoundly and close your mouth and pinch your nostrils together. Now exhale as best as you can and as forcefully as possible. This increases the pressure inside your chest and airways, and this stimulates the vagus nerve.

Given that your vagus nerve densely innervates these areas of your body, this technique is an excellent way to stimulate it.

Yoga Chanting and Yoga Poses

Activate the Diving Reflex

The diving reflex refers to the way our body reacts when plunged into the water. Blood flow increases to our brain and our senses become sharper. You don't need to jump into the water to recreate this. Simply splash your face with cold water all the way up to your eye line, and you'll feel the effects of this.

Another way of recreating this effect is to hold a pack of ice cubes against your face and hold your breath for a second. A third method is to drink water and play around with it as it flows over your tongue as you feel its texture.

Yoga

Yoga is an ancient exercise practice that originates from ancient India. It is a physical and spiritual practice that places great emphasis on learning the mind to body connection. If you really wish to get into yoga, I highly recommend locating a qualified teacher who can walk you through the various poses as well as the breathing techniques to follow.

Speaking of breathing techniques, let's look at the first practice you can follow to activate the vagus nerve.

Half Smiling

Smiling is a valuable social tool, and your ventral system plays an essential role in enhancing it. The connection works the other way as well, just as it does with socialization. Forcing yourself to smile is a great way to signal to your brain that there is no threat in the immediate environment, and it removes you from the dorsal or sympathetic nervous state.

This isn't a yoga practice, and you can do this wherever you are, as you go about your day. Move your mouth into a half-smile, and imagine your jaws loosening. You can close your eyes if you want when doing this.

Opening the Heart

Sit down on the floor and close your eyes. Bring your hands to your shoulders and inhale deeply. As you inhale, open your chest and raise your head and simultaneously rotate your shoulders outwards. As you exhale, turn your shoulders back in and lower your chin into your chest.

Perform this movement a few times and make it as smooth as possible. This relaxes the muscles in your neck and lower head and, as a result, relaxes the nervous system as well.

Warrior Pose

The warrior pose isn't a terribly complicated pose, but it is best if you learn the posture from a teacher who can explain the intricacies of it to you. The pose brings your breath and body into sync and forces you to ground yourself to the earth. It also tests your ability to balance and is a great way to start off your day.

Cow Pose

You can perform the cow pose by kneeling down on a mat and then supporting yourself on all fours as you extend your hands out in front of you. Tuck your stomach in as you inhale and bend your neck inwards. As you exhale, let go of your belly and arch your back and shoulders down as you look upwards.

The vagus nerve innervates your belly, and as a result, this pose helps activate it.

Metta Meditation (Loving-Kindness Meditation)

Metta refers to loving-kindness, and this form of meditation has been shown to place the mind in a state of mind that promotes peace and love. The meditation itself is straight forward. Close your eyes and take a few deep breaths to ground yourself in the present moment. Once this is done, visualize all the people in your life and send them all the love you have and wish them well.

Then, visualize someone you don't know and have never met and send them the gift of your love. Visualize yourself, showering them with all your love and compassion. Practice this for five minutes and observe the difference in your mental state. From a biological perspective, loving-kindness meditation helps remove yourself from a country where a threat exists to an environment where you are safe and secure. This naturally helps activate the ventral system.

Yoga Nidra

Nidra is usually the culmination of all yoga practice sessions. To do this, you simply lay down on your mat or on the floor with your palms facing upwards. Observe your breath and the sensations in your body. Practice this for around 10 minutes or so.

Other Factors That Stimulate the Vagus Nerve

The following factors aren't confined to yoga or any particular exercise method but nonetheless have an effect in stimulating the vagus nerve. Where applicable, I'll highlight research that supports the benefits of these methods. You can and should implement all of them immediately

Singing

I've already asked you to hum, so you might as well sing at this point. It doesn't matter how atrocious you are, and singing helps you activate the vagus nerve. Just like humming, the key is to truly let yourself go and sing at the top of your voice. Medically speaking, this stimulates the muscles at the back of your throat and helps activate the vagus nerve better.

Meditation

Like yoga, meditation is a practice that originates in ancient India.

Meditation's benefits extend well beyond stimulating the vagus nerve. Meditation has been shown to literally change your brain and rewire it to create a greater sense of calm. As far as anxiety and depression are concerned, the increased awareness that meditation brings can be a problem since it will make the problem appear worse at first.

The key is to have a strategy in place beforehand that you can carry out. Remaining detached and observing or reinforcing positive habits at this juncture are examples of things you can do to implement change.

Laughter

Laughter is extremely beneficial for your well-being, but you don't need me to tell you that. A study conducted on people practicing yoga laughter (an exercise where you throw your hands up and laugh as hard as you can) found that their Heart-Rate Variability decreased. As you've already learned, HRV has a direct correlation to vagal tone. The lower the HRV, the higher the vagal mood, and the better health you are in.

Prayer

A study conducted on those performing rosary prayers found that their vagal tones increased. The exact reason for this is not known. There is speculation that counting the beads produces changes in the breath and that this is the cause of increased vagal tone.

Pulsed Electromagnetic Field Therapy

This method involves sending electromagnetic waves through the body with an aim to stimulate bodily function. A study conducted on healthy, middleaged men found that PEMF therapy resulted in increased vagal tone. You can buy devices off the shelf that provide such stimulation.

Probiotics

As mentioned, the gut microbiome plays an essential role in regulating your mood and the consequent anxiety and depression levels. Probiotics help with this, but keep in mind that most supplements are of no use. It's far better to consume fermented foods such as yogurt or sauerkraut to help with digestion.

Exercise

Perhaps the best medicine of them all for anxiety and depression. Exercise and physical movement challenges you and gives you a sense of accomplishment, which directly opposes the miserable feeling that depression causes. In case of anxiety is your issue, exercise gives you an opportunity to vent your frustration at something.

Exercise also releases endorphins in your system and helps you feel better. All in all, there is no downside to exercise, and you should aim to make it a part of your daily routine.

Massage

A massage is a form of visceral manipulation, and a full body massage relaxes you entirely and removes any blocks in your body. Certain types of massages directly stimulate the vagus nerve and are incredibly beneficial for your health.

Fasting

Fasting helps the body regulate the production of ghrelin in your system, and this helps regulate your blood sugar as well as your metabolism. In addition to this, practices such as intermittent fasting help you lose fat and increase muscle tone, which enables you to become healthier.

Sleeping on Your Right

Research is pretty limited with regards to this, but there is anecdotal evidence that is sleeping on your right increases vagal tone. There's nothing to lose by trying this out to be honest.

Recommended Foods

Seafood

Seafood happens to be rich in Omega 3 fatty acids that play an essential role in diminishing free radicals within our system. Free radicals are a blanket term used to describe chemicals that cannot be flushed out by the body on its own. They've been linked to the existence of cancer and other autoimmune diseases.

Fiber

Fiber helps with excretion and improves gut health. Given the gut to brain connection, consuming fiber in your diet should be a priority.

Sensory Deprivation

Sensory deprivation is a method that has been increasing in popularity lately. The technique is best suited for people who do not have claustrophobia, and there is significant research that suggests that the technique works exceptionally well.

To begin with, the method itself is pretty straightforward. It works by immersing yourself in a highly concentrated salt and magnesium bath. This allows you to float in the water entirely without any aid and thus creates a sense of weightlessness. Your eyes will be covered, and you will shut the lid of the tank on top of you. Keep in mind there are also open-air tanks that don't have caps for those of us who like a little bit more breathing room.

Daily Practices for Activating the Vagus Nerve

- Gargling 2x daily: Keep a cup to your sink. Use it to rinse your teeth twice a day, in the morning and at night.

- Gag reflex activation 2x daily: Use your toothbrush to activate the gag reflex on both the left and right side of your soft palate, as you brush your teeth in the morning and at night.

- Humming 2x daily: Practice humming deep in your mouth during your daily commute, or to note your day. You can use the term "om" to keep the pulse as long as you can exhale in your throat.

- Cold shower 1x daily: End your daily shower with cold water for one minute (as cold as possible) and practice breathing through the temperature change shock. It becomes easier to increase the time every three days by 30 to 60 seconds until all of your showers are taken under cold water.

- Deep breathing 3x daily: Before each meal, perform three to five minutes of deep breath in a quiet room. This will help calm you down for each meal and improve your digestion.

- Sunlight exposure 3x daily: Go outside and expose your skin to the sun within 30 minutes of sunrise, in the middle of the day, and within 30 minutes of sunset, at least five minutes each time. If you live in a colder climate, expose your eyes to the light for two to three minutes at each of these times and practice breathing through the cold whenever you do so.

- Sleep on your side each night: Put a pillow in between your knees to prevent you from sleeping at night on your side.

Meditative Techniques for the Support of the Vagus Nerve

We've already tackled some of the great benefits of mindfulness meditation. It can help you focus on your present moment and make you more aware of your body. It can bring awareness to physical sensations you would have ignored before. All of this can help you further understand your physical reactions to stress and how to bring relaxation to your body. There are many different ways you can approach meditation. Choose the one that you're the most comfortable with.

One mindfulness meditation that can help with stress, anxiety, and depression is loving-kindness mindfulness. This is because it creates more positive emotions, which, in turn, change your body physiology and help you improve your vagal tone. Loving-kindness can help you overcome any issues with low mood or low self-esteem. They can also help you with emotions like anger, guilt, and resentment. All of these involve our feelings about ourselves or others. Loving-kindness is about reminding yourself of kindness to you and others. It creates so many positive emotions that it can change your mentality and is a great way to start improving your cognitive distortions.

To start your loving-kindness meditation, you're going to need a safe, comfortable space. Since this meditation is kind of long, you may want to have this book open while you do it, or you can listen to a guided meditation to walk you through it. This loving-kindness meditation is based on the work of Dr. Emma Seppala.

Start by sitting cross-legged if you can or sitting on a chair. Relax your body, and close your eyes so that you are focused on your inner world, rather than the external one.

1. Take a deep breath in and slowly release it.

2. Think about someone who is close to you and loves you. This can be someone from your life now, someone from the past, or someone who has passed away. Imagine that person standing beside you.

3. They are sending you their love and their hopes for your happiness and safety. See and feel the warm wishes coming from that person toward you. You might picture it as a wave coming toward you,

filling you, and surrounding you.

4. Think about a second person who also loves you. They also send you their love and their hopes for your happiness and safety. See and feel that warmth surrounds you and enter inside of you.

5. Now, imagine that you are surrounded by all the people you have ever known who love and cherish you. Your friends, family members, and community are sending you their love and their hopes for your happiness and safety. Surround yourself in that love and fill your heart and body with it. You are overfilled with love.

6. Look at the first person beside you. Start to send them your love. You and this person are alike; you both wish for happiness and love. Send your love and your hopes for their pleasure and safety to them.

7. Silently repeat this phrase three times, sending the wishes to that person.

   - May you be safe, may you be happy, and may you be healthy.

8. Now focus on the second person on your other side. Start to send them your love. You and this person are alike; you both wish for happiness and love. Send your love and your hopes for their pleasure and safety to them.

9. Silently repeat this phrase three times, sending the wishes to that person.

- Like I hope to, may you live a good life full of safety, happiness, and good health.

10. Now imagine all of the other people who love you. Start to send them your love. You are all alike; you all wish for happiness and love. Send your love and your hopes for their happiness to them.

11. Silently repeat this phrase three times, sending wishes to those people.

- May your life be full of happiness, well-being, and health.

12. Think of an acquaintance that you know. Someone that you have no particular feelings toward. You are all alike; you both wish for happiness and well-being. Send all of your hopes for their well-being to them.

13. Silently repeat this phrase three times, sending the wishes to that person.

- Just like I hope to, may you live a good life with health and happiness.

14. Think of another acquaintance who you know, but don't have any particular feelings toward. You are all alike; you both wish for happiness and well-being. Send all of your hopes for their well-being to them.

15. Silently repeat this phrase three times, sending the wishes to that person.

- May your life be full of happiness and well-being.

16. Now imagine the whole world in front of you. All of the living beings in the world are just like you;

they all want to be happy. Send all of your warm wishes to them.

17. Silently repeat this phrase three times, sending your wishes to every living being in the world.

- May your life be full of happiness and well-being.

18. Gently bring your awareness back to yourself. Take a deep breath in and then out. Bring awareness to your body and mind. Think about how you feel after doing this meditation. Open your eyes and continue your day.

Once you've completed the meditation, you should feel a little better. You may feel relaxed and calm. You may even feel more compassion for others. If you don't, that's okay. Keep practicing loving-kindness meditation to gain the benefits from it. If this isn't your cup of tea, try some other kinds of meditation. If you want a more physical sort of meditation, try yoga, qigong, or taiji (Thai chi).

Yoga is often considered relaxing as it uses movements and breathing to help calm the body. It can sometimes be triggering for people, so if you've experienced trauma or PTSD, proceed with caution or do yoga with someone who understands trauma. There is some evidence that yoga can stimulate the parasympathetic nervous system and the Vagus nerve. It's also been linked with helping to heal depression, anxiety, stress, and chronic pain. So it can be worth it to try if you want to activate your Vagus nerve.

There are a lot of different types of yoga to try. If you've been practicing yoga for a while, stick with the ones you know or try something new. If you're a beginner, then don't start with the advanced classes.

Here are some significant types of yoga that are good for beginners but also help with stress reduction:

Hatha Yoga - In a hatha yoga class, you'll have a basic understanding of the different poses in yoga. It's generally considered to be a gentle yoga class and shouldn't strain you too much. You'll learn to work on posture, while also following the breath.

Iyengar Yoga - This type of yoga is very focused on your position and poses. There isn't a lot of strenuous work, but you'll have to maintain poses for a while. The classes should be run by someone who understands the human body well and can provide you with support in different positions. If you choose to do Iyengar yoga, make sure that your instructor has been welltrained and can provide you with the necessary guidance, so you don't hurt yourself.

Restorative Yoga - Like the name itself suggests restorative yoga is all about relaxation. In this style of yoga, you put yourself in poses while being supported by other materials. So while you are in the pose, you're not straining yourself.

Each of these kinds of yoga can require a class with an instructor. However, if you don't want to go to an actual level, you can find some good yoga videos online. For relaxation, choose yoga videos that use terms like gentle yoga, beginner's yoga, or yoga for relaxation. Find videos that you enjoy and help you relax. If gentle yoga is not your thing, they try vinyasa yoga, ashtanga yoga, or Bikram yoga. All of these are more intense, but also put a lot of emphasis on the breath and movement. All of them can help you achieve more balance in your body.

Qigong is a new type of meditation. It combines physical form and movement with focused breathing and meditation. Its goal is to balance your life energy or Qi. It has a lot of backing from both traditional medicine and modern science. Many scientists consider qigong to promote well-being. It causes relaxation of your muscles, reduces your stress levels, and deepens your breathing, which has been repeated many times thus far and can help with activating your Vagus nerve. Qigong has many different forms, and it can be adapted for many different people. It's often used medically in China, is related to many kinds of martial arts, and is sometimes just simple meditation and movement. One of the most popular forms of qigong in the U.S. is tai chi.

If you've ever walked through a park in a major city during the weekday morning, you may come across a group of people doing slow, fluid movements that look very much like martial arts. They're most likely doing Thai chi. It is, in fact, a type of martial arts that focuses on the body's slow movement and breath. It is considered a style of meditation, even though there is an exercise component to it. If you're interested in either qigong or tai chi, find a class near you and give it a try. You can also find videos on YouTube for home practice.

Tai chi takes a lot of practice before its flow becomes routine, so keep working with it.

Practical Exercises to Stimulate the Vagus Nerve

The Power of Stretching

Let's talk about stretching. This doe tie into yoga, but if you combine diaphragm breathing with yoga. Doing this as you do a mall stretch will benefit you in a ton of different ways. For starters, most people don't stretch nearly enough, and it shows. Most people aren't flexible, and it affects how they end up faring in life. Many get injured due to a lack of stretching.

But it's more than that. Stretching is powerful. Stretching is used to help naturally stimulate the body, and make movement simple. There is a lot you can get from this, and you can get out of this. Most people don't realize that they're not only releasing tension within the muscles when they stretch, but they're also focusing their breathing, so it's simple and yet very useful.

A lot of people don't stretch enough, so that tension sits there. But, a way to naturally start up the parasympathetic nervous system and activate et vagus nerve is to do just this. Sitting down, stretching out your body, and working on this helps promote relaxation and wellness, and from there will stimulate your entire body in its way.

Plus, it feels fantastic too. Most people don't stretch enough, and they'll realize as they do this, that they need to. Sometimes having calming music, and focusing on your breathing changes this.

You also don't have to hold the stretches for very long. About 10-12 seconds suffices.

Try touching your toes, stretching your arms behind your head, pushing them up, and holding your arms in the air, or even just moving towards your foot will help with this. There is a lot of benefits to be had with stretching and a lot of beautiful things to do with this. You'll be shocked, you'll be amazed, and most of all, you'll be quite happy with the power of this small exercise. You'll feel invigorated for whatever is to come for you in the future.

Consider stretching right before you begin your day, or at the end of the night, and see how it helps you feel during the day. You'll feel your vagus nerve stimulate almost immediately.

Weight Training

Weight training might seem weird to do to stimulate the vagus nerve, but it does work. That's because, when you lift weights, it is changing the speed of the body. Plus, through the power of repetition, you get your body to relax. A lot of people think lifting weights is only for big, burly people, but that isn't the case.

Ever just doing a few sets of curls will change the way your body feels, and your vagus nerve. Many people also think they need to start with a heavyweight right away, but that isn't the case. I suggest just progressively overloading over time if you want to see physical gains. You must understand that weight training is a relaxing process, and you must breathe as you do it. You need to breathe in deeply to help with pushing the oxygen around to help you with strenuous exercise. So yes, pick up that dumbbell and try it. You'll feel the difference right away.

HIIT Workouts

HIIT, or "high-intensity interval training" is a form of workouts that require you to do a lot in a minimal period. Sometimes, this involves sprinting; other times, this can be pushups, sit-ups, or other exercises. The main goal behind this is to do a lot in a bit of time, and through spurts.

These sprits are what cause vagus nerve stimulation. The vagus nerve is usually not stimulated if you're always stressed out. Still, the periods of stress, and then relaxation kick the vagus nerve into gear, helping it activate whenever needed.

HIIT workouts are also great because they are often straightforward to do. No matter what it is that you do, you'll feel the difference in these immediately.

A lot of people don't realize that HIIT is also very short in terms of workouts.

Some people can get these done within a half-hour or so, and that's their workout for the day. But HIIT is great because it lets you get a great workout and also lets you improve your wellness and health.

It's a great way to get in shape, so it's something you should consider if you're looking to improve your physical fitness.

Walking

Walking is an excellent option if you're not going to the gym to lift or don't want to spend time doing HIIT or yoga. Walking is an excellent habit to get into because it stimulates your body and helps with physical fitness and wellness. Your vagus nerve will get stimulated with walking, especially if you live a sedentary lifestyle.

I think walking for 30 minutes a day is ideal, especially if you're unable to do this otherwise. Sometimes, pacing while on your breaks is a great way to do this, and walking also lets you improve on your health and wellness.

You want to do this to help with your physical fitness, and walking is a good start, especially if you're not active otherwise.

Jogging is also another good one because this can help with deep breathing. A lot of people, when they start, will get into the habit of breathing with short breaths, but that won't work here. This can make it hard to run, and you might pass out. With jogging, you want to make sure that you're breathing in a slow, deep, and even manner, and focus on this. This will help with your vagus nerve and help you get into the habit of breathing deeply. You can also do running with this, but it's more high-intensity and might be harder to engage in deep breathing otherwise.

Jumping

Again, another form of cardio that's great, but your vagus nerve will love it. Jumping jacks, burpees, and other jumping exercises are useful because they help improve circulation, which can help with blood pressure and your vagal tone.

When you jump too, be mindful of your breathing. Try to do it with a deep breath, and you'll notice it's a much harder workout, but you'll feel the difference. It increases blood flow, blood pressure, and heart rate as well.

Your vagus nerve will thank you for this, and you'll be able to, with jumping too, improve on your health and wellness.

Aerobics

Aerobics is another higher-intensity exercise, but some variants aren't as extensive or intensive as others. Zumba tends to be on the more intensive side, but there are different classes you can try. However, there are even different kinds of aerobic exercises, such as water aerobics, weight training, cycling, and even yoga.

All of these, when combined, are wonderful for vagus nerve stimulation and are great for the body. You'll be amazed and surprised at how helpful this can be for the body, and how you can use these to help improve your vagus nerve. They encourage you to breathe during these too, which promotes deep breathing and thereby vagus nerve stimulation.

Swim it Out!

Swimming is a great aerobic exercise too, and if you're not a fan of jogging or running, or weight training, swimming is good.

That's because it helps in many different ways. For starters, you're submerging your head, which stimulates the mammalian diving reflex, which includes your vagus nerve. It also pushes you to control your breathing as you move. You need to hold your breath, but also walk through the water, and it's a combination of both of those things which provides you with the correct vagus nerve stimulation.

It also will help improve your bodily movement. That's because you're moving about, and this encourages blood flow too. You'll notice that as you begin with this, it's hard to do, but over time, you'll get better with this. It's a beautiful form of cardio, and it's gorgeous for properly stimulating the vagus nerve.

Dancing

Finally, we have dancing. Dancing is an excellent form of self-expression for starters. Even if you're silly, it can help you feel much better about yourself. Dance is lovely because it enables you to improve your physical fitness, get the blood flow moving, and help you stay active and fun.

There are so many different kinds of dance classes these days too. You can do Zumba or other forms of dancing. Some people even like ballet dancing because it requires control, and this can stimulate the vagus nerve. They're fun to do, and they encourage you to move, control your breathing, and let you express yourself.

Even silly interpretive dancing helps. After all, if it can make you laugh, that naturally stimulates the vagus nerve, and that's a beautiful, fun way to do this.

Dancing is excellent, and it lets you feel good about yourself. Consider dancing the other time you want to express yourself correctly and feel good.

When it comes to stimulating the vagus nerve, these are all practice activities that boost the vagus nerve. Your vagus nerve is vital because it lets you relax the body and helps curb inflammation. But, while these exercises are great for stimulating this, it also helps with getting the body moving, which increases vagal tone. It can also help offset obesity, diabetes, and other conditions related to weight.

Your vagus nerve does benefit from exercise, and here, we tackled why and how it happens, and the benefits of this.

Vagus Nerve Stimulation to Heal from PTSD

Stimulating the vagus to stop the sympathetic system is done when the individuals feel safe and secure. The following activities can instantly promote varying levels of these feelings.

Make connections with others. It is challenging to feel as if you can trust others. The best way to switch from the sympathetic nervous system to the parasympathetic nervous system is to make a connection with someone else.

Hug. Along with the first technique, hugging helps us feel safe and connected to others. By giving or receiving a hug, you can instantly trigger the vagus nerve.

Laugh. If hugging is not your thing, you can laugh instead. Laughing can help stimulate the vagus nerve to release oxytocin. Oxytocin encourages you to make connections with others and lift your mood. Laughing, just like hugging, helps you feel connected with others and can strengthen bonds.

Shake it off. One of the ways you can bounce out of the shutdown mode is to do a full-body shake. Before you go into a full out shake, do a quick body scan. Are there any areas of your body that feel tense or stiff? If you find tension in your body, these are the areas you want to focus on when you wiggle and shake. Give your attention to each area as you shake the tension out when you have gone through all the fields and feel relieved, pause for a moment to take in the stillness that surrounds you and let it fill you. This is your body waking up again. This is the feeling you want to recall when facing a trauma-induced memory or episode.

Daily Long-Term Vagal Toning Technique for Trauma and PTSD

Healing from trauma or PTSD can be a life-long process. Strengthening the vagus nerve daily results in developing the skills necessary for your mind and body to bounce back from traumatic events and experiences that trigger trauma symptoms. The following regular exercises you can perform to receive long-term benefits from the vagus nerve:

1. Bhramari pranayama. The Bhramari pranayama is referred to as the humming bee breath in yoga practice. This type of breathwork helps you tone the vagus nerve by stimulating it through the vocal cords. When you perform this breath, you can

keep the nervous system calm and prevent it from going into fight or flight mode. To achieve this type of breathwork, get into a comfortable sitting position on the floor or bed. Cross your legs and bring your hands to cover your ears. Your thumbs should face down towards the ground. Take a deep breath in; as you exhale, begin to make a humming sound that vibrates through your ears. You can repeat this process as many times as you need.

2. Sleep on your right side. Trauma and PTSD have severe adverse effects on sleep, and how you sleep can add to these difficulties. Sleeping on the right side of your body can stimulate the vagus nerve and lead to a more restful night's sleep. You should avoid sleeping on your back as this is often the worst position for vagus nerve stimulation.

3. Tai chi or qigong. Like yoga, tai chi and qigong are forms of slow movement

exercises that stimulate and tone the vagus nerve. These practices focus on strengthening the internal systems through precise moment and breath. Sun Style tai chi is a type of tai chi that utilizes smooth, flowing movements that can help individuals feel grounded. This is an essential aspect for those with PTSD who can often feel lost and unsure of where they are, resulting in panic, frustration, and confusion. Doing a simple Sun Style tai chi sequence can tone the vagus nerve and be an effective way to help heal from trauma.

Sample Short Form Sun Style Sequence:

Step 1: Begin at a standing position with the elbows near your side, slightly bent upwards. Palms should face in towards each other. On the exhale, lower your arms and your bend your knees slightly, then lift the arms back up as you take a step forward on the left foot. Push your hands in front of you as you bring the right foot up to meet with the left. Feet should be slightly apart.

Step 2: Bring the hands back slightly towards the chest, palms facing one another. As you inhale, move them wider apart; on the exhale, push the palms back in towards each other.

Step 3: Step the right heel slightly up and out to your right side. Allow your weight to shift to the right leg as you turn your palms to face out in front of you. Push the palms forward, then extend the arms around and out to your side. Your gaze should follow the left hand. Then bring the palms back around in front of you, so they face each other again while stepping the left foot up to meet the right. Bend the arms, so they are at a 90-degree angle in front of you. Fingers should point toward the ceiling.

Step 4: Move the right hand to meet the left elbow. Step your right foot out to your right side as you move your right hand to extend in front of you, palms facing away from your body, and the left arm comes down. Shift your weight from your right leg to the left leg as you turn the upper body slightly to the left and move the right arm down somewhat to your side while lifting the right wing with the palm facing away from your body. Bring the left foot closer to the right and repeat this process two times.

Step 5: Bring the hands back slightly towards the chest, palms facing one another. As you inhale, move them wider apart; on the exhale, push the sides back in towards each other.

Step 6: Shift your gaze to the right hand as you stretch it out in front of you while the left hand comes to meet the right elbow. Step your left foot out to your side as you reach the right hand up towards the ceiling. Turn the left palm to face the floor and push down towards the ground. Your weight should be on the left foot. Turn your body slightly to your left as you move the left hand to sweep across your left knee and bring the right hand towards the right ear's side. Push the palm of your right hand forward and deliver the right foot in just barely to meet the left.

Step 7: Bring the hands towards the center of the chest, so the palms are facing each other (about 6-inches apart). Move the right hand forward as you step back on the right foot. Keeping the weight on the right foot, bring your left foot back to meet the right as you move the right hand back and bring the left hand forward.

Step 8: Step forward on the left foot while turning the palm of the right hand up toward the ceiling and the left palm down toward the ground. Shift your weight to the right foot as you move your right palm out in front of you and the left palm back toward your abdomen. Bring the right foot forward, stepping in front of the left while reversing the palms so the remaining faces towards the ground and the right up towards the ceiling. Shift your weight to the right foot as you move the right hand back towards the abdomen, and you left out in front of you. Step the left foot in front of the right as you make your hands into fists and bring the right-hand level with the left.

Step 9: Bring the left foot back slightly. Un-fist your hands and turn the palms, so they are facing out in front of you. Step back on the right foot as you push the hands forward. Shift your weight to the right foot and bring the sides back in towards your body.

Step 10: Turn the palms, so they face one another. On the inhale, move them wider apart; on the exhale, push the hands back in towards each other.

Step 11: Repeat all the above steps but start on the reverse side.

Vagus Nerve Stimulation to Heal from Trauma

The body experiences other distressing signs of post-traumatic stress— a tightness in the abdomen, a sinking sensation in the stomach, a familiar pain in the mouth, or a constant sense of fatigue. We now understand that as part of the recovery process we have to turn to the body and as a result, we have seen an increase in the use of meditation, mindfulness, tai chi, qigong, Feld ink circle, massage, Craniosacral therapy, dietary therapy, and acupuncture for post-traumatic stress disorder.

Such mind-body treatments are helping us to be less passive, less aggressive, and less impulsive to stress. We're growing our understanding of the options we need to make us stay grounded and relaxed. We felt in need of this more. One way the mental-body treatments operate is by activating the nerve in the vagus. Awareness of how this nerve works offers a profound understanding of traumatic stress and promotes our healing capacity. The vagus nerve has, therefore, taken center stage in the treatment of trauma.

"Mind-body treatments work on the nerve of the vagus to help you regain the balance—some breath and movement activities in this article, aimed at relaxing and resetting the vagus nerve. By a cycle of self-study and conscious body consciousness, you will continue to develop techniques that help you regain a sense of comfort and recover from trauma." Effects of Mind-Body Therapy Vagus Nerve Yoga Dr. Arielle Schwartz. The utilization of mentalbody therapy is correlated with a wide variety of wellness and wellbeing changes, including physical and mental wellbeing enhancements Reduction. They allow us to focus on our feelings, impulses, and behavioral motives. This observational capacity tends to improve tolerance to discomfort, which can reduce emotional reactivity, fear, panic, chronic pain, and depression. Mind-body treatments improve self-understanding and the capacity to perceive that person's point of view with understanding.

Moreover, mental-body treatments are successful as they require structural improvements in the autonomic nervous system as determined by increases in vagus nerve activity. The vagus nerve reaches through the muscles of the nose, inner ear, chest, back, lungs, stomach, and intestines from the brainstem down. Mind-body treatments make changes in how we relate to our surroundings by encouraging a gentle look and allowing us to try new breath or activity patterns that communicate specifically with other parts of the body. Researchers also calculate the changes that exist in the vagus nerve, which is often referred to as respiratory sinus arrhythmia by heart rate variability (HRV). HRV refers to the rhythmic heart rate oscillations that arise with the breath. It's a function of the intervals between beats in the heart. Higher variability in heart rate is associated with a better ability to withstand or rebound from stress.

In comparison, lower variability in heart rate is correlated with stress and anxiety. You should think of any form of mind-body therapy that improves the heart rate variation by creating strength and endurance within the autonomic nervous system. As a result, switching between emotions of anticipation and easiness is smoother.

Pain and recuperation of the vagus nerve vagus and pain. If we feel a threat (real or perceived), we change the way we breathe. We can get a good picture here by considering the ways animals react to predators. In certain situations, an animal may rapidly breathe into the upper chest, which is a protective reaction of the nervous system that allows them to run or fight in a dangerous environment. In other situations, an object may freeze that includes breathing shallowly or holding the air to prevent a predator from being detected. This freeze reflex causes the animal to stand very still and is a response to the threat of immobilization. For certain situations, animals are weak, and a predator, not a scavenger, can lose interest in a dead animal. An evolutionarily older vagus nerve axis supports both the freezing and sluggish responses as a member of the parasympathetic nervous system.

Most notably, an animal can activate the stress reflex by shaking and breathing in a manner that maintains homeostasis until it's healthy. Nevertheless, we humans will also live for long periods either in high activation (fight and flight) or weak activation (freeze and faint) responses. This appears to be the case where abuse is persistent and prolonged, as in the case of Complex PTSD (more of this can be found here). We frequently miss the resources to handle challenging or painful experiences. It may result in physical stress and restricted breathing habits that form the foundation of our posture, modes of activity, and general self-sense.

The Vagus Nerve and Trauma Therapy

To help repair the vagus nerve, you will learn practices; but, not all training is right for everybody. Alternatively, I encourage you to play with and try a range of methods of breathing and action before you discover what fits for you. You will start developing techniques through a cycle of self-study and conscious body consciousness that help you maintain a sense of protection and recover from trauma. Here are a few tools to help get you started: Attend your Gut: Dr. Arielle Schwartz Somatic Therapy. You can also boost the health of the vagus nerve by ensuring a balanced digestive system. The inner nervous system, also known as the belly brain, is comprised of the "microbiome" that resides in the gut. This habitat includes hundreds of healthy and bacterial organisms that live within the intestinal tracts. An imbalance in your intestine can result in an inflammatory reaction in your immune system and cause a wide range of debilitating symptoms, including anxiety and depression. By raising the sugar intake and finding any latent food intolerances, you will build a balanced microbiota. You may require a doctor or nutritionist to help find the causes of a deficiency in the gut; however, the effort it takes to incorporate these improvements into your life is well worth it.

Conclusion

Chronic pain and inflammation is a terrible condition to live with. Still, as everything has shown, there is hope in the incredible power that the vagus nerve holds. The truth is that vagal stimulation is still in its infancy. Research is continually being carried out and the areas of potential research. As mentioned, merely scratch the surface of the full body of new studies that are being undertaken. You can expect this decade to bring rapid advances in the field of chronic inflammation remedies, and the vagus nerve is likely to be at the front and center of it. Living with pain is severe. It's even worse when you realize that all those pills you're popping aren't doing anything for you and are mere placebos. It is a position in which my wife and I found ourselves at different points in our lives. Thanks to the miracle that is the vagus nerve, we managed to dig our way out of it. Challenges in life never cease, but living with pain, inflammation, and chronic illness is one particular challenge you don't have to deal with day in and day out. While the vagus nerve is a miraculous thing, it helps to live a healthy lifestyle. As you can see from the alternative methods to stimulate the vagus nerve, the majority of solutions point towards living a balanced and overall healthy lifestyle. This is precisely what ancient wisdom teaches us, and we would do well to follow it. Methods such as yoga and meditation might not find an excellent fit for themselves in today's reaction based medicinal approaches. Still, when it comes to being proactive with regards to your health, they remain amongst the best solutions to undertake.

So take action starting right now and begin implementing the stimulation exercises mentioned. Stop thinking of yourself as a machine that needs to be fixed and is thinking of yourself as a living being, the product of thousands of years of evolution. Your body is perfectly adapted, in some sophisticated ways, to survive and thrive here on planet earth. It has far more healing power than you may have ever given it credit for. While its design may not be perfect for handling social media interactions or supporting you forty hours a week in your office chair, it's designed is perfect when supported by a whole and healthy lifestyle. Please don't blame yourself or your body for its physical, psychological, or emotional shortcomings. Instead, work together with your body to gain autonomy over your wellness. One of the benefits of vagal stimulation is that as your mood improves, you'll begin to believe in the treatment to a greater extent. This will create a self-reinforcing positive cycle!